GRACED:
Finding Healing in a Hurting World

Pamela J. Bradley, EdD

All Scripture quotations marked NIV are from The Holy Bible, New International Version. Grand Rapids: Zondervan Publishing House, 1984.

Cover art by Louise Bishop, friend and talented Muskogee artist along with creative graphic artist, Brooke S. Edwards.

Yorkshire Publishing
3207 South Norwood Avenue
Tulsa, Oklahoma 74135
www.YorkshirePublishing.com
918.394.2665

Dedication

This book is dedicated to the many strong and caring women who have encouraged, guided and influenced my life in positive ways. It is also dedicated to my husband and best friend, Charles, who constantly supports and encourages my many endeavors.

May God use these stories to help the hurting people in our world find healing and forgiveness through Him. May all be Graced with His love!

Acknowledgements

A big THANKS to Maudye Winget, dear friend and former colleague, my daughters, Bekie and Cali, as well as my sisters, Hope, Phyllis, Paula, Karen, and friends, Katherine Winniford and Dianne Haralson for providing revisions and input into how to best pen the heart of these true accounts.

Thanks to the unnamed women who shared their testimonies (you know who you are)! May your stories inspire and encourage others to find forgiveness through Him.

Introduction

"Then Jesus said, "Come to me, all of you who are weary and burdened, and I will give you rest."
Matthew 11:28

L ove. Healing. Grace.

In this book, you will read about six women who came to Jesus with an emotional burden – Guilt. Each exchanged this burden for freedom, peace, love and grace.

Too often, we feel undeserving and become our own worst enemy. We forget that life is less about chance than it is choice. At times, we can't let go of our past and find ourselves unable to move forward. We accept the shame and the labels society casts our way and allow our guilt to define us.

Guilt often causes us to forgo what God has offered; not because it must be earned, but because our human misconceptions *refuse* it when we feel unworthy.

Though we ask forgiveness and receive it, we decline to let go of our baggage, repressing a burden that can take a tremendous toll on our well-being: emotionally, physically, and ultimately, spiritually. Clinging to this load pulls us away from God. Not because *He* has moved away from us, but because *we* have moved away from Him.

Most of us know well the scripture, *"For all have sinned and fallen short of the glory of God,"* Romans 3:23. Yet, when we fail to move beyond our sin, we allow that heaviness–that guilt which is conveyed through insecurity, anger, apathy, or animosity to guide our lives. This rejection can cause us to miss that *release–*that *freedom* we desperately seek when we fail to accept and experience the glorious significance and power of Christ's death on the cross: **Forgiveness.**

I pray the experiences in these women's lives serve as a balm for you to dissolve the guilt that keeps you enslaved. May these accounts restore your heart, renew your mind, and resolve your circumstances so that you, too are receptive to what God has already made available for *all* of us: Love. Healing. Grace: an occurrence that is full of an encompassing kindness and incredible wholeness which initiates a new sense of self worth.

"If you, Lord, kept a record of sins,
Lord, who could stand? But with you there is forgiveness,
so that we can, with reverence, serve you."
Psalm 130:3-4

The Unnamed Women

All of the women in these stories are purposely unnamed. This is so their stories may resonate with you in your own unique, but possibly similar situations.

All true accounts, three chapters include modern women who courageously chose to share their experiences. With contrite hearts, they approached God's throne to seek His mercy and discovered how vast and caring our Saviour is as He provided healing to each.

The other stories may be familiar. They remain true to scripture, yet are shared through the possible voices of the three biblical women who headlined them: the woman at the well who drew living water to quench her thirst; the adulteress, who discovered eternal life instead of a death sentence, and finally, the prostitute, whose tears allowed Jesus to cleanse her heart as she washed His feet.

My hope is that these women make an emotional connection with you as you discover their commonalities. All were sinners. All were under a social microscope. All were judged by the world, judged by themselves and condemned. Yet, Jesus provided love for all.

All six women were in great need of a healing that could only be found through God's grace. All felt shame and sought acceptance that the world refused to give. Through His forgiveness, they found wholeness and discovered self worth.

Your Turn

The final story is yours to tell. Your testimony, your healing, and your journey is a way for you to share with others how God has manifested His Grace in your life. To build your story, you'll find at the end of each chapter a place (Heart to Heart) to record your thoughts and reflections.

From these notes and your experiences, *you* are encouraged to write chapter 7. As you construct your own personal testimony, may you experience the same peace these women found. Through prayer and commitment, may this opportunity bring you freedom from any guilt that attempts to characterize you. May your testimony bring you closer to knowing and experiencing God's healing, His limitless love and may you be *Graced*, as these six women were!

Table of Contents

Chapter 1
Held Hostage

"Come to me, all you who are weary and burdened, and I will give you rest. Take my yoke upon you and learn from me, for I am gentle and humble in heart, and you will find rest for your souls. For my yoke is easy and my burden is light."
Matthew 11:28-30

The radio crackles before settling onto a clear station. She slows while driving through the construction, unaware that the caller's tale in the broadcast seems to mirror her own. And then she hears it. In the woman's voice, she hears *her* story: *her* regret … *her* remorse … *her* sorrow ... *her* choice … *her* sin … *her* secret. She pulls the car to the shoulder and allows the tears to flow freely, her mind going back to that fateful day … thirty years ago.

Her shoes stir up dust as she jogs down the road. The dust is nothing compared to the stir about to happen if her "sin" is discovered. Nausea tingles her nostrils, and she winces at the tenderness in her breasts. She cranks up the music already blaring through earbuds and picks up the pace—as if she can outrun this. Heaving near the side of the road, she wipes her mouth with a wristband, realizing remorsefully "it" has caught up with her.

"Mama, what should I do?" she whispers aloud. It's a silent prayer to her mother who died too soon. Still bent over with hands on her knees, a passing car honks and she jumps, startled back into reality. It's been five years since her mother's death, yet she still mourns for such a confidante. She shakes her head and starts the slow jog home.

Strands stray from a damp and sloppy ponytail as she enters the house. Mopping the sweat from her forehead with a towel, she gulps a large glass of water and pauses to think. Despite keeping busy, the loneliness always finds her when her children spend the required monthly weekend with her ex-husband.

She tidies the already clean kitchen and sweeps the floor … again. Time has not eased the difficulties that came with divorce. And she finds no support from the majority of the rural, Bible-quoting townspeople, who treat her as an outcast.

In the bathroom, she reads the directions on the box while awaiting the shower water to warm. Following those directions, her eyes widen as she stares down at the red cross slowly forming on the white tube in her hand. Positive!

Stepping inside the tiled stall, she sinks slowly onto the floor and sobs. Snot mingles with tears in the steamy shower and it seems like hours before she rises.

Wrapping a towel around the long, brown strands hanging limply about her shoulders, she twists them into a tight knot, like the one in her gut. A splotchy blurred face stares at her from the fogged mirror and she clears it with a wad of toilet paper. *"Crying doesn't help. It only makes me uglier,"* she whispers to the red eyes staring back from two sides of a nose swollen twice its size. In less than an hour, her children will return home. What will she tell them? What will she tell anyone?

Her divorce a year ago had been hard enough. After years of trying to be the "good girl," her world came crashing down when her husband had taken company with another woman, leaving her a single mom. She had found it difficult to financially and emotionally support her little family, but somehow, she had managed.

Right after her husband left her, she had attempted to reach out to a few people in her community, but the "churched" ladies weren't having it. Her "scarlet letter" became apparent when she attempted to broach the subject of divorce with her women's worship group. Each of the young women had been assigned to share a story using significant scriptures.

Starting with Psalm 15:16, "Turn to me and be gracious to me, for I am lonely and afflicted," she felt compelled to speak of the isolation she felt as a divorcee. Following with a brief summary of the book, *I've Got to Talk to Somebody, God: A Woman's Conversations with God,* by Marjorie Holmes, she wrapped up with Psalm 147:3, "He heals the brokenhearted and binds up their wounds," hoping the women in the room might feel so inclined.

Instead, her words were met with stone-cold silence and several icy stares, while a few women looked away as if doing so might make her and the topic disappear. Others coughed or cleared their throats, uncomfortable. The awkward stillness was deafening.

Finally, the spectacled, older woman leading the group smiled stiffly and clasped her hands as if to close off the subject while dismissing her. "Well … thanks for sharing. Now ladies, don't forget the potluck lunch being served today, immediately following the sermon. The food and pies just smell so yummy!"

As the women filed past her in pairs and trios, most moved around her as if divorce might be contagious. She was left alone sitting in the cold, brown metal chair. Their contempt was clear. "But why?" she wondered. "I am simply a *divorcee*." She finally rose, picking up her purse along with the remaining fragments of her heart, and walked out, feeling numb.

After collecting her children from their classes, she walked purposefully to the parking lot, refusing to look back. She knew she would never enter these doors again. The support she needed would not be found within these walls, or even more disheartening, within these people.

Returning to the present, crazy thoughts began to fill her head. If she was treated that way over her divorce, what might it be like once her new "sin" was discovered? Would she lose her job? If so, how would she support her children, who were already traumatized by divorce? She sucks in a deep breath returning to her original question. "Who can I tell?"

"No one," she says aloud to *no one* as the room reflects what she feels inside … empty. She rubs her temples, pressing a thumb into one eyeball where a migraine is beginning to form. Guilt settles like a black cloud in her heart and her head feels full of concrete. While dragging a comb through her wet hair, she silently prays. She must keep and hide this sin within her heart.

The front door bursts open. "Mom! Mom? Where are you? We're home!" Her young son's voice breaks through the gloomy and quiet state into which she has settled. She swallows hard and exhales, hoping to calm her rattled being.

"In here," she calls from the bedroom. Little heads bob through the doorway, and she smiles, opening her arms to receive their sweaty, puppy-dog-smelling hugs. *"Ohhh! I missed you!"* she squeals, kissing their cheeks and heads.

She laughs as her children reveal their weekend adventures, all the while experiencing an emotional tug-of-war as her new burden yanks at her heart. She chokes back a sob and forces a cough when her daughter looks up. *How will they fare this next disgrace?*

Over the next two weeks, she continues praying. Despite the prayers, her usual confidence in God is lacking. Stained with shame, she wrestles with imagined comments from the community: *"What a bad mother! What a terrible influence for her children!"* After wiping a thousand tears from their faces this past year, she lacks the strength and energy to do it again. Frankly, she realizes she lacks the fortitude and faith as well, and so she makes her decision.

On a rainy, windy Friday morning, she drops the children off for their weekend with their father. After driving to her sister's house, she spends the next hour in a long and painful conversation before they head together to the doctor's office. The car is quiet and tense until her sister punctures the silence with a question, "Is there anything else I can do?"

"No," she blurts harshly while shaking her head like an angry child, bent on following through despite any consequences. Resentful—as if God is responsible for her plight—her mind is set. Since no words will change her predicament, she speaks none and the rest of the drive to the city falls into a thick and heavy silence. Neither she nor her sister speaks what's on their hearts.

Inside the doctor's office, her sister reaches up to hug her. At first, she resists, but then gives in, looking down through tear-brimmed eyes. She is thankful for her sister's loyalty and unconditional love. Then she turns and hesitantly hands the forms back to the receptionist, feeling as if she has just signed her soul to the devil.

The door slams loudly behind her and an intolerant nurse points to the gown on the table. Her tone hateful and her eyes glaring, the nurse roughly hooks up the IV, all but voicing, "Birth control was a better option, don't you think?!"

Knowing the nurse's harshness was intentional but deserved, she grits her teeth and swallows. Ironically, such treatment only strengthens her resolve and she is determined to appear decisive and strong. Her tears betray the façade as she drifts into Never-Never land.

In a fog, she opens her eyes, blinking from the bright lights about her. The nurse unhooks her IV and demands, "Get dressed. It's done."

The pain in her gut bites when she moves, but not as much as the thoughts in her head as her heart cries, *"Murderer!"* Tears splatter on the tiled floor while she dresses. She signs off and the nurse dismisses her.

With no protest, she walks unassisted to the waiting room. Her sister insists on holding on to her as they walk to the car. She refuses a hug, feeling unworthy of one. She declines to speak during the ride home, not wanting to relive this experience. She wants to curl up and die, but that's not an option; not with her children dependent on her.

Unable to undo *this deed*, she wonders how she will live with herself. Her throat aches and her eyes feel dry, as pins seem to be poking through them. Her heart pounds rapidly as if to prevent the decaying of her soul. Never has she felt so low. So forsaken. So empty. Not only does she believe she has given the devil her own soul, she feels she has given him two.

She spends the weekend with her sister, hoping to escape the pain. Words cannot console her, and she wonders if she will ever awake from this nightmare. Her dreams are haunting and bizarre, and she discovers there is no relief, even in sleep. She draws her knees up tightly, curling into a fetal position as she cries softly, dying inside. Her sister stays close, bringing her soup, bringing her water, and bringing her love.

Equating her self-worth with her deed, she feels her connection to God has been severed. Not because He left her, but because *she* left Him. She feels too unworthy to call upon His name and too shameful to pray. She dares not show herself to God at this time. *Will I ever be normal again?* She wonders.

Stumbling through the next weeks, she allows a numbness to overtake her. She realizes that if it weren't for her children, she would will herself to die. But she knows they need her and that abiding purpose keeps her going.

Refusing to be a part of any encounters, emotions or conversations related to her experience, she *does* survive as the days turn into years. Her secret, stuffed into a deep, dark place in her soul, remains contained. She refuses to face it, thus refusing forgiveness. The guilt is still raw. The memory is too heavy. So, she ignores it, keeping it safely hidden inside, a hostage in her soul.

Until one fateful summer afternoon, on a long, solitary drive, weary from too little sleep, she flipped through the radio stations, hoping to find peppy music to keep her awake. Instead, she heard the raspy voice of a 60-year-old woman repenting on a Christian broadcast. The woman's words eke with sorrow, and her message paralyzes, causing her own hand to freeze when attempting to change the channel.

As the woman's voice on the radio catches her breath between sobs, so does she. The elderly lady confesses a secret which has kept her an emotional prisoner for decades. "Forty years ago," the woman wept, "I had an abortion. This deed has haunted me for years. It has eaten up my soul, and I am tired of carrying this. Today, I am 60 years old, and I want to be free of it. I've never told anyone all this time. I guess I was too ashamed. And so, I'm asking for God's forgiveness on a public broadcast." she sniffled and blew her nose, "I think there is someone else out there just like me. They need forgiveness, both from God and themselves. And they need to ask for it just as I am. I am so tired of carrying this burden … I've held it for far too long. I just want to be free."

With each circumstantial detail belted from the radio, the torment becomes *hers*. She, too has experienced those fears: unprepared, alone, fearful of humiliation and rejection, and ill-equipped to face the unknowns of her predicament. Her lips began to quiver and her body began to quake, a prelude to the emotional dam about to burst.

In the older woman's confession, she hears *her* own regret, remorse, sorrow, choice, secret and sin. They share the same guilt. She pulls off the road because of her emotional state and for the next hour, wipes tears from her face as quickly as wipers remove rain from a windshield during a torrential downpour.

Her remorseful words are incomprehensible, but she knows God is making sense of them. When she can finally speak, she prays aloud, hearing her own confession. *"Forgive me, Lord. Forgive me for taking the life of my unborn child ... for choosing to have an ... "* It takes everything inside her to finally say it, *"... Abortion!"* As the word comes from her mouth, it is shrill. She has let it go.

She begs forgiveness in every possible way as she senses God's presence in the darkness. *"Bring your burden to me and I will give you rest."* She knows He has said it before, but this time, she not only hears Him, she experiences His wholeness as she allows Him to remove the "yoke" of oppression she has carried too long. She is no longer hostage to her deed. As her tears continue to flow, the guilt is released. She senses the Spirit's peace. She experiences God's grace. She feels Christ's love. At last, she is free.

"I finally get it, Lord. No good deed of mine could ever buy redemption. Nothing but your blood could bridge that sinful chasm which has separated me from You! You called me years back to experience your love, your grace, your forgiveness, but I refused, feeling unworthy. Yet, if I could have earned my way to Heaven, then Your death on the cross was in vain. Thank you for giving me grace and mercy!" She recalled a phrase she had once heard *"God's Grace is always bigger than any sin,"* and this time, she accepted it.

Heart to Heart:

"But you are a chosen race, a royal priesthood,
a holy nation, a people for his own possession, that you may
proclaim the excellencies of him who called you out of dark-
ness into his marvelous light."
1 Peter 2:9

What dark secret is holding you hostage? What is keeping you from God's grace? What sin do you need to let go of to experience His peace? Remember, there is nothing you can do that Christ's mercy can't redeem. He is greater. He is mightier and His position is more powerful. His ways are more loving. You will never *earn* or *deserve* God's grace, *but* you may receive it if you only ask, if you only accept. His blood has paid your fee.

_____

_____

_____

Chapter 2
Drawing the Water of Life

*Jesus answered her, "If you knew the Gift of God and who
it is that asks you for a drink, you would have asked him
and he would have given you living water."*
John 4:10

"What do you mean *living water*?" the woman contemplated. Thus begins the longest biblical conversation with Jesus ever recorded!

Never mentioned by name, this Samaritan woman was taken aback when Jesus chose to speak to *her*. After all, Jesus commits several taboos (according to the Jewish customs of that era) to interact with this *woman. He* spoke to a woman who is not in the presence of her husband—a definite no-no in that time! Worse, she was a woman of mixed-race ... a Samaritan, a people the Jews considered to be second-class. Worse yet, the woman was a moral outcast, scorned by her own people. And He later drank from this impure woman's cup, making *Him* (according to their beliefs) as lawfully and ceremonially unclean as she.

The woman was alarmed at Jesus' presence, a man at the well during the hottest time of the day. After all, it was typically the woman's task to draw water, and most did so during the cool of the morning. So, why was He here? What did He want from *her*, a Samaritan woman?

Jesus breaks the silence. "Woman, will you give me a drink?"

Uncertain of His intent, the woman at the well looked about, wondering if another person might be present. Finding no one, she surmised from His attire and dialect, and responded. "How is it that you, a Jew, ask *me*, a Samaritan woman for a drink?" She knew Jews did not associate with Samaritans, believing they were beneath them. She also knew most Jews avoided this area, concerned with racial conflicts or fearful that ceremonial desecration could result from an interaction with a Samaritan.

Jesus *did not*. He took this path knowing full well that on this sweltering afternoon, He would encounter *this* woman at Jacob's well. In fact, Jesus sent His disciples on a quest for food because He wanted time alone with her, so that she might speak openly with Him. Awaiting her daily routine, Jesus watched for this moral outcast to trudge toward the well where He sat.

His wait was not long. As she neared, He could see the woman's condition was much like the clay jar she carried; thick-skinned and rough from the wear and tear on the outside, but hollow inside. Only shame filled the vacated walls of her soul.

Preferring to draw water in the scorch of the mid-day's sun rather than face the scorn of her people, the woman was careful to avoid rocky encounters. She was cognizant that her shell of a heart might shatter due to its fragility.

As she lowered her jar to draw water, she was startled when Jesus spoke to her. "Please give me a drink." He wiped the perspiration from His brow and waited.

She paused and Jesus smiled, aware of her naiveté. "If you knew the gift of God, and *who* it is who asks for a drink, you would have asked me and I would have given you *living water*."

"What do you mean *living water*?" the woman at the well contemplated. It was her turn to smile as she points to his empty hands. "Sir, you have nothing to draw water with and the well is deep. How and where will you get this living water?" She scoffed as she continued. "Are you greater than our father Jacob who gave us the well and drank from it himself ... as did his sons and his livestock?"

Jesus gestured toward the well, "Everyone who drinks of *this* water will be thirsty again. Yet, anyone who drinks of this water I offer will never thirst again. The water I give will be like a spring of water flowing inside them. It will bring them eternal life." Jesus' words are extending to her His grace, His mercy, His forgiveness, but the woman only regards the literal sense.

The woman considered this notion. *Never thirst again?* Searching Jesus' face for signs of mockery, she only saw kind eyes looking back at her. And so, she dared to respond, "Sir, give me this water, so I will never be thirsty nor have to come all the way back here to draw water again." The thought of not having to haul water back and forth was quite appealing, and avoiding the taunts of her people even more alluring.

Jesus looked to the woman and extended an invitation. "Go. Get your husband and come back."

A small breeze blew, stirring the dry, red dust about them, just as His invitation roused the guilt inside her. She dropped her head, her cheeks warming with shame. She was unsure how she should respond. Finally, she looked up and whispered, "I have no husband."

Jesus slowly nodded, not in an accusatory manner but in agreement. "You are right when you say you have no husband, for you have had five. That much is true. Yet, the one you live with now is *not* your husband."

Sweat now dripped from her brow. She smoothed back a piece of hair threatening to spill into her face and tilted her head with a false haughtiness. Her eyes squinted into the sun as she forced herself to look up at Him. *Is He judging me just as my own people do?* Bracing herself for the criticism she'd become so accustomed to, she attempted to re-route the conversation. "Sir, I can see you are a prophet. Our ancestors worshiped on this mountain, but you Jews claim that Jerusalem is the place where we should worship."

At this, Jesus gently shook His head, and shared truth and grace while he considered her heart. "Woman, believe me. The time is coming when you will not have to be on this mountain or in Jerusalem to worship God. You Samaritans worship something you don't quite understand, something you do not know." He extended His hand upward. "We worship what we know, since salvation is from the Jews. Yet the time is coming, *and* that time is here, when true worshipers worship the Father in spirit and truth. These are the people the Father wants to worship Him. Since God is spirit, those who worship Him must worship in spirit and truth."

With that misconception, the woman responded to what she *did* understand, "I know that the Messiah, the one called Christ, is coming. When He does, He will explain all things to us." She nodded her head for emphasis.

Jesus leaned toward her, declaring a great secret, "I who speak to you am *He.*"

For a moment, she didn't get it. As His words sank into her empty soul, excitement filled her body. She felt her heart pounding wildly inside her chest. She laughed nervously, afraid to believe what she had had just heard. She looked into the eyes of Jesus and knew He was speaking truth. She was oblivious to the harsh stares of Jesus' disciples who had just returned. Their eyebrows were raised, and they glanced back and forth from the Samaritan woman to Jesus and back again, wondering why *He* would be talking to *her*.

The atmosphere engulfed in silence, she felt the disciples' stare upon her. No matter. Her gaze returned to Jesus, her Messiah. A nervous laugh escaped her ... this time with relief as Jesus' eyes gleamed with the remarkable truth He just shared with *her*. The judgment of the disciples and of the world did not matter. She was **free!** The suffocating shame was gone, replaced with a hopeful new start in life.

She turned and ran the half mile back to town, forgetting her jar at the well. She wanted to share the living water she had just received from Jesus with the world!

Waving her hands as she entered the town, she cried out to anyone who would listen. "Come! Come quickly! You've got to see this man ... this Jew! He spoke to *me*! He told me everything I ever did! Could this be the Christ? The Messiah?" Her voice professed more truth than question.

Her excitement was met with skepticism. The people looked at her doubtfully. What was she babbling about now? They shook their heads and turned back to their business.

But, the woman did not stop. Her enthusiasm was contagious, and her testimony piqued their curiosity, even if she didn't quite convince them. And so, they dropped what they'd been doing to follow the woman back to well to see this man she spoke of.

At the well, the people discovered what she had found ... The living water. Jesus. Her freedom had led them to find theirs (John 4:4-42).

Jesus' actions sent a timeless message that love transcends all barriers: race, gender, and socio-economic status. His grace is greater than all our sin. His forgiveness is more generous than any of man's religions, laws or moral dictates.

Yet, because of her concern with her own unworthiness, the woman at the well almost missed God's grace. Slow to grasp Jesus' message, she nearly waived His redemption, His mercy ... His grace. She came close to bypassing the healing that finally set her free.

Heart to Heart:

What is inside your jar? Is it empty, just waiting for God to fill it up? Or are you storing up guilt and shame from sins committed long ago that keep you feeling unworthy? Let go of those sins and draw from Jesus' living water. Drink in His peace and forgiveness. Allow yourself to experience whole love and healing through prayer. Jesus is waiting for you in a quiet place where just the two of you can visit honestly. He invites you to openly share all that is on your heart and mind. He is inviting you to drink of that same living water. All you have to do is ask. Write down what your soul needs to empty from that worn and weary jar so that God can fill you up with His love and grace.

"... You do not have because you do not ask God."
James 4:2

_____

_____

_____

Chapter 3
Giving Up the Wheel

"He will cover you with his feathers, and under his wings you will find refuge; his faithfulness will be your shield and rampart."
Psalm 91:4

On the coffee table is a gun ... a .45 Colt staring up at her, promising to put an end to this sudden and unbearable pain. She fingers it, and contemplates. Unused prescription pills sit beside the gun, inviting their own morbid escape.

She sets the revolver aside for a moment, twists off the cap of the pills and peers inside. "No ... too drawn out," she whispers, returning her attention to the handgun. "This is quicker!" The cold metal promises an easy out to life's betrayal, and as she reaches for the gun once more, her thoughts return to an earth-shattering day, just two years earlier, when their marriage had begun to unravel ...

It was in the deep south, where her husband was stationed with the navy. They were still mourning his younger brother's suicide a month before. Their drug of choice to dull the pain came in the form of alcohol.

This action brought harsh consequences when she and her husband were arrested for public drunkenness and spent part of the night in jail. She still felt shame just thinking about it, and was mortified when her mother found out. Her mother's sharp counsel was seared into her brain.

"You are responsible for your actions and you cannot blame others. In spite of hard times, you decide whether you'll be a victim or a

victor. You can grow bitter or grow better through life's experiences. Now get it together!"

Shortly after that night, she prayed off excessive drinking and begged God for forgiveness and mercy. She was done with this wild, destructive life.

They moved back to her husband's tiny home town and she felt God had given them a fresh start. She committed to start anew. Her husband verbally abused her, placing his blame on her for his unhappiness. Yet, she made a vow to work harder and was determined to make their marriage work.

Their box-shaped house, which sat off the main street of the tiny shot-gun town, was just a dilapidated two-bedroom. The only love the 50-year-old house ever received was her fervent cleaning attempts and the ignored pleas to pull and replace the stained carpet on the floors. Garbage piled up on the side of the house, where a make-shift pit served as trash service since her husband refused to pay for it.

Living beneath her standards was her choice, one she embraced for love; the same love that forced her to forgo her remaining college education to work at a local café and other temporary jobs so she could follow him wherever the navy sent him. Deep within, however, she sensed what seemed to be a warning; change was coming.

Leaving the mom-and-pop-grocer one night, she was caught by surprise as a sudden gust of cold wind whipped across her face. The brick walls of the store were highlighted briefly by a harvest moon as twirling dead leaves decorated the parking lot. It brought an uneasy feeling … an unrest in her soul.

Ignoring it, she gripped the bag of groceries more tightly and walked purposefully to the car, driving the two short blocks to what she now called home.

She entered the house, using one arm to hold the door as the other hugged the shifting bag of food which threatened to spill to the floor. She smiled at him and wondered why he just watched and never offered a hand as she placed the bag on the counter.

She eagerly embraced him, throwing her arms around him as she planted an affectionate kiss on his lips; a daily ritual she'd begun when he returned from work. He remained stiff, cold, distant, and his blue eyes held no trace of the love from last night. Her lips stung, betrayed by his withdrawal. "We need to talk" he said coldly.

She sighed and shrugged, giving into his frequent melodrama. "Sure," she replied, beginning to arrange groceries into the cabinets.

"Sit down!" he commanded gruffly. His tone alarmed her.

"I'll stand," she replied, tightening her fingers firmly around the can in her hand as if it held hope, despite the forewarning in the pit of her stomach.

"Fine," he responded, leaning casually against the sink as he mumbled to the floor, staring at the tiles. He shoved his hands into his front pockets. "I want a divorce."

She dropped the can onto the floor, narrowly missing her foot. Yet, she didn't flinch. Her world just stopped.

The temper tantrum that ensued came from deep within … from the despondent young woman who patiently gave into his every whim throughout their six-year marriage while putting her own life on hold. She grabbed the wooden chair in front of her and threw it to the floor, stomping her foot with a challenge. "No!" she cried out, much like a defiant two-year-old.

His face seemingly grew old and tired before her eyes as he waved her off. "There's no arguing this."

She stood in his path as he attempted to leave the kitchen. "Why?" her eyes flashed with angry hurt.

"You don't listen," was his only reply.

"That's it? That's all you have to say after I gave up everything to follow and support you?" Her eyes filled with tears.

His eyes and voice were hollow as he spoke, "You'll be better off. You'll find someone new … someone who deserves you."

"No!" she protested. "I married you and I'm not quitting. I took my vow seriously … 'til death do us part.' Remember?" she argued.

Her cries fell on deaf ears as he walked out of the house, grabbing his truck keys, and muttering, "You can have the house." And with that, he was gone.

She sank slowly into the worn fabric on the green couch. Tears skimmed her arms as they streamed from her burning cheeks. She felt sucker-punched as she screamed to the walls surrounding her, "What just happened?!"

Shattered, she attempted to recover from the shock. She wondered if God was punishing her for previous deeds as she stared down at the coffee table.

Back to this horrific moment, the .45 stares back, promising to put an end to this sudden and unbearable pain. She fingers it, and contemplated. Unused prescription pills sit beside the gun.

She pictures her mother crying and shakes her head. She can't do it. She can't do that to anyone. She shudders and stifles a sob. In her head, she begins praying, knowing she must give this to God.

Her new reality is harsh and cold. She lacks direction, but prays, telling herself she'll have to suck it up and live with the pain—if only for the sake of her family. She places the gun back onto the table, her ears ringing at the beeping of her phone. Shaking the fog away, she answers.

It is her older brother, inviting her to dinner. She accepts, casually adding as she walks into the bedroom to throw clothes into a bag, "I think I'll spend the night at your place—since my husband just asked for a divorce." She speaks as if she is discussing tonight's dinner menu, her heart and faith transitioning to survival mode.

She doesn't pack much; wanting few reminders of what once was. She stashes two suitcases of clothing into the trunk and places a few absolute necessities, including every legal document she can find (upon her brother's sound advice) along with her childhood Christmas ornaments – plucked fresh from the still-standing tree – on the seat beside her.

Driving the dusty dirt road, she smokes cigarette after cigarette, singing loudly to the radio in an attempt to drown out the negative reminders in her head. Smashing a cigarette into the ashtray, she mumbles, "I've got to give this habit up," referring as much to her crumbling marriage as the smoldering pile of ashes flickering in the tin holder.

Two days later, her secret is out and her whole family knows. She remains at her brother's home for two weeks, despite the invites from her mom and sister. She remains in a stupor, like a zombie searching for meaning and a reason for all this. Her consolation comes in the form of something familiar and destructive, alcohol. She accepts shot after shot, not caring what happens to her, and half hoping something does. She just wants to numb the pain since she feels that God isn't moving fast enough. Her reasoning is fragmented, just as her heart is, and her soul feels void.

Her stomach is in knots, and she resorts to triple layers of clothing as her weight drops significantly. She doesn't care. She just wants a way to suppress the clawing, curling, screaming riot inside. Her worried mother secretly calls a family conference, determining an intervention. It is decided she will recover best if she stays with her sister, a state away from the many memories of what was.

Again, she packs her sparse belongings: two bags of clothes, a few books, photo albums, gas money, and $50 for a new life journey. Her hands go numb and begin to cramp up when she grips the steering wheel tightly as she drives down the road. She tries to focus on simply breathing in and out, refusing to succumb to the threatening anxiety attack as she leaves the state. Hours later as she nears her sister's home-town, she prays to God as she navigates the traffic, feeling as if this hot, crazy maze mimics her own life.

Upon arrival, her sister fishes out a camera and insists on taking a picture. As she protests, her sister interjects, promising, "Don't worry. One day you'll look back at this picture and laugh to you see how far you've come." She rolled her eyes at her sister. She seriously doubted *that* day would *ever* come.

Every weekday, after fitful nights wrapped in constant prayer, she is roused from her warm bed with the cold reality of her new life. Every morning, her sister cheerfully greets her with a cup of steaming, creamy coffee, inviting her to work out. And each time, she responds with a curse and pulls the covers over her head to shut out the world, accepting a victim mentality. "It doesn't matter. Nothing matters. The world hates me and so does God!"

Finally, on a particular pitch-black night that seemed to match her soul, God reaches out to contradict her. While smoking a long-saved cigarette on the roof of the tiny apartment her sister had helped her secure, she spews another angry prayer to God. Clenching her fist so tightly toward the sky that it hurt, she realizes she *must* let go of this anger and pain that seems to suffocate all she had hoped and meant to be.

She hears her phone ring, causing her to almost fall off the rooftop where she was sitting as she jumps to answer it. "Who would call me at *this* time of night?" she wonders, when she hears her baby brother's voice on the line. She double checks her watch, surprised he's up this late as it's a school night.

He tells her he could not sleep. He tells her God placed it on his heart to call her and relay a simple message, a message well beyond his 14 years. "God still loves you and He just really wants you to know that." She chuckles sarcastically, wondering how he could know what is going on in her head and heart right now. He repeats the message, making sure it is relayed loud and clear.

She sucks in her emotions and manages a feeble response, "Thanks, little brother. Good to know." She hangs up the phone and looks to the sky, the stars sparkling wondrously around her. She smashes the half-smoked cigarette in disgust. The timely message was received.

She realizes she allowed her husband to be her total focus for the past six years. She followed him everywhere and allowed him to lead her down such a destructive path. She knows it wasn't his fault. It was her choice; misguided by blind love. But, that doesn't lessen the pain.

Before climbing in bed, she turns on the ceiling fan. The air flow causes something to blow from the top of her dresser. Picking it up, she views the skinny woman slumped over in the picture. It is her, two months earlier, when she arrived at her sister's house.

She is tired of this picture. She is tired of what she's become. She is tired of the direction of her life.

Feeling defeated, she tosses the picture, watching it land inside an old bag beside her dresser. Climbing into bed, she pulls the blanket around her shoulders, and feels it envelope her like a warm hug. It's been so long since she's been hugged by anyone other than her sister.

The depth of her loneliness causes tears to spill from her eyes. In desperation, she prays. "God, I'm so tired. Please help me. Please let me hear you. Please let me feel your love. If you really exist, please let me know. I'm so tired of being angry. I've hit rock bottom and I just can't go on this way." Her quiet sobs finally subside and the only sound is the whirring of the ceiling fan. As she lies in the darkness, she hears a faint whisper, "I've got you, daughter." She opens her eyes and blinks, scanning the dark room. The only movement comes in the form of the spinning blades above. Settling back into her pillow, she continues to pray quietly. And then she senses His presence … a peace and well-being pulsing through her veins, bringing a renewed sense of worth. She buries down into the blanket, forcing a whispered "Thank you, Lord," while vowing to draw close to Him again. She remembers her baby brother's message, "God wants you to know you're loved." She closes her tired eyes, falling into a deep sleep, resting more soundly than she had in months.

The following morning, she acts upon her promise, determining to feed her malnourished soul with His word. Delving into daily devotionals and scriptures to lift her spirits, she feels an energy she hasn't known in weeks.

As her habits change, so does her mindset. The prayers and scriptures sink deep into her very fiber, providing her with a slow and steady strength and a renewed hope as the days turn into months.

By spring, she discovers a bolder, more confident faith, a peace and joy she hasn't experienced in years. Little does she know how much she will need this—God's armor—in the very near future.

As summer passes uneventfully, she is thankful for a reprieve from hardships. However, fall does not bring the same. In late October, she packs up her things from work and stuffs them in the passenger seat of her car. The bags overloaded, a couple of paper items fall to the floorboard. No matter—she'd pick them up when she arrives home.

Buckling in, she spies her phone peeking out of the top of her purse. Several missed calls from a former sister-in-law. Her sixth sense kicks in and she knows something is wrong. Praying as she taps in the numbers, she hears condolences immediately pour forth from a familiar voice. Her dreaded fear is confirmed. Her ex-husband is dead … shot through the heart, a suicide, just like his little brother.

After allowing almost an hour of tears, anger and remorse to flow freely, she wonders if she is equipped to deal with this next crisis. With her head pressed against the steering wheel, she spies the papers on the floor. One is the picture her sister took of her the previous year. A reminder of the gaunt, empty, shell-of-a-person she used to be. Beside it is a scripture she had scribbled down on a scrap of paper weeks before, *"So do not fear, for I am with you; do not be dismayed, for I am your God. I will strengthen you and help you; I will uphold you with my righteous right hand"* Isaiah 41:10. It was God's voice … His commitment to her.

As she grips the steering wheel, a resolve floods through her entire being. Allowing God's promise to sink in, she senses the difference in her response to this new predicament. She has placed God in the driver's seat. He is not punishing her for past sins, and the guilt that too often consumed her in the past, is gone. Satan would not win this battle.

Though the recent news brings a deep sadness, she embraces the comfort and grace with which God surrounds her. Knowing she doesn't have all the answers, she knows she must move forward in faith.

Unsure of how she'll navigate this next valley, she welcomes God's presence beside her … all the way. Leading her, loving her and restoring her. Leaving the photo on the floorboard, she folds the scripture into one hand. As she puts her car in gear, she looks up to the sky and whispers, "Here we go, Jesus. Take the wheel." Pulling onto the highway, she feels His voice inside her heart.

"I've got the wheel, daughter. More importantly, I've got you."

Heart to Heart:

*The Lord is close to the brokenhearted and saves those who
are crushed in spirit.*
Psalm 34:18

How can you turn any detours into victories? What trials, tough decisions or hardships have worn you down? Are you spiritually malnourished? What might a current photograph of your heart reflect? How can you allow Christ to restore your faith ... in Him and His plans for you? How will you allow Him in the driver's seat so that He may steer you to a place of peace, strength and grace? Though the terrain is rough, the Lord is strong and He will guide and love you through all things.

_____

_____

_____

Chapter 4
No Stones

When they kept on questioning him, he straightened up and said to them, "Let any one of you who is without sin be the first to throw a stone at her."
John 8:7

S he caught her breath. She could not feel the oxygen in her lungs. The woman looked up at Jesus as He spoke. Horrified, anxious, exhausted, frightened and fearful, her heart was heavy with guilt. Hauled through a mob the night before, the dust in the air was heavy with condemnation. As dawn approached, she was pushed through the crowd and made to stand before Jesus with disgruntled men surrounding her.

Disgraced, the adulteress held her breath, waiting for Jesus to pronounce her death. Dragged to the temple courts by the Scribes and Pharisees, the woman's haughty accusers had skipped the entitled trial, as well as her opportunity to confess her wrongs. She was captive through the night, enduring cruel taunts and ridicule … disdain and judgment.

Tears streamed down her dirty, flushed cheeks and she lowered her eyes. Her accusers demanded Jesus throw the book at her as they scooped up their stones. Their goal was to trap both her *and* Jesus, though she was unaware she was but a pawn in all this. She only knew her very life hung in the balance as they shouted insults her way.

She looked about, wondering why her "partner-in-crime" wasn't dragged before the court, just as she was. After all, he willingly chose to lay with her. Was he not guilty, too?

A sob escaped her throat when the angry mob demanded an answer of Jesus. "Teacher, this woman was caught in the act of adultery. By law, Moses commanded us to stone such women! What do you say?"

They waited, expecting an answer. When Jesus remained quiet, they continued questioning Him. Still, He ignored their demands and stooped to write in the sand as if He couldn't hear them. He realized their main objective was to trap *Him* using the woman, so instead, He scribbled a condemnation toward her accusers.

The adulteress glanced toward the ground at this man they called Jesus. Her head bowed in shame, she wondered how and why He ignored them. As she waited for what seemed hours, she jerked when the stillness was broken by the religious leaders' insistence that Jesus come to a decision.

Wiping the dirt from his hand, Jesus rose to speak. His stoic gaze pierced their very souls as He panned the crowd, settling on some of the most prominent leaders. *"Let any one of you who is without sin be the first to throw a stone at her."* Jesus stooped again to write in the dust.

The Pharisees were silenced. They knew the Sabbath prohibited *all* work … whether it be writing more than two words (*unless* on the ground, as Jesus was lawfully doing), *or* picking up stones. More importantly, though, they realized Jesus had turned the tables on them. The accusers became the accused.

The woman caught her breath. She looked up at Jesus as He completed that statement. She squeezed her eyes shut, crumbling into a ball on the ground as she placed hands over her head, bracing for the pain of that first stone, and ultimately her own death. Moments seemed an eternity before she finally dared to peek through one eye, wondering why no rock had struck her. Incredulously, she watched as one by one, the elderly men dropped their stones and walked away. The younger men followed suit.

The woman's tears turned to silent sobs of relief until only Jesus stood. She gasped again. Would He throw the first stone?

Instead, He asked softly, *"Woman, where are they? Has no one condemned you?"*

"No," she whispered in disbelief, still unsure of His intentions.

Jesus reached down, pulling her gently from the ground. *"Then neither do I,"* He declared. *"Go now and leave your life of sin."*

She rose cautiously, tears spilling from her face. Though she would have liked to embrace Him, she did not. The norms of that time would not allow it. The shock of what just happened settled in, and she fled, fearful that He or the Pharisees would change their minds (John 8: 2-11).

She knew she had escaped death, but more importantly, as she ran, she realized this Jesus had granted her much more. He had provided her with forgiveness. He extended His grace, and with that came His unconditional love and a new life.

Jesus exhibited wisdom, mercy and power in this instance. Not only does He point out how His love transcends man's legalism within religion, but He reminds us that in a world of blame and shame, He came to save, not condemn (John 3:17). Neither then should we.

Christ's grace superseded to allow this woman to find freedom through forgiveness, and healing from condemnation and certain death. As Jesus spared the woman's earthly life in that moment, He also gave her eternal life.

Heart to Heart:

Christ calls us to love Him first and then our neighbors as ourselves (Mark 12:31). So, while many of us may do well with the first two, we often struggle with the latter ... loving self. How can you love yourself as God does, so that you might allow His forgiveness to heal you? What stones are weighing you down? Who is casting them your way? How can you allow Jesus to free you from the world's judgment? Write down what guilt is burdening you. Then give those stones to Jesus and rest on Him. He is *the* Rock.

> *"For God did not send his Son into the world to condemn the world, but to save the world through him"*
> *John 3:17.*

_____

_____

_____

Chapter 5
Worthy in My Father's Eyes

The teachers of the law and the Pharisees brought in
a woman caught in adultery. They made her stand before
the group and said to Jesus, "Teacher, this woman was caught
in the act ... ."
John 8:3-4

"Y ou're nothing but a whore! A lying, easy whore!" The slap from her father's broad hand doesn't sting nearly as much as the accusing words or the disdainful look contorting his red, angry face. "You weren't raped!" he reproaches. "You just couldn't say no, could you?!"

Her protest, silenced by his raised hand, is ignored. Squeezing her eyes closed, she cannot bear witness to the horror of his deed. Her clinched fists flail at her father's fleshy bulk, but the physicality is too great. Attempting to remove herself emotionally from this moment and this bed, she cries out as her father's naked, sweaty body weighs on her.

As she continues to protest, her father finally stops, shoving her away, off the mattress and out of his life. Relieved, she almost runs from the room, grabbing her crumpled clothing off the floor; but not before his words stab her heart once more.

"I thought you'd grow up to be like your mother! But you're not! Do you hear me?! She was a lady, but you're nothing but a whore! Allowing *some* backwoods boy to have his way with you! Get out of this house and don't come back!" he shouts. She complies, forcefully closing the door behind her. Longing for a hot shower to scrub the filth from her body, she is fearful of further retribution. She grabs her suit-case, quickly throwing in clothes, and leaves.

Attempting to process what just happened, she calls a friend, who drives her to the bus station. She feels dirty, disgusted, unworthy – even deserving of her father's contempt. In survival mode, she heads for a grimy restroom in the corner of the bus stop and proceeds to wipe down her skin with wet paper towels. The restroom reeks of urine, bringing on a strong sense of nausea, which results in violent heaving. She stares at the vomit in the toilet, relating it to her current sense of worth. Tears spill over her bruised cheek and splatter into the foul-smelling bowl below.

She hears a call for her bus over the intercom and wipes her mouth with the damp paper towel. Flushing the toilet, she enters the next phase of her life: lost, alone and pregnant.

Following her daddy's orders to terminate "this iniquity," (as he referred to it), she obediently boards the bus, prepared for a long ride. She recalls her father's response to her confession. No sympathy. No hugs. Just a harsh condemnation and a look of revulsion as he shook his finger and stated, "You'll never be like your mother or your sister!"

She knows that in her father's mind, her older sister is perfect: wiser, prettier, more educated, and most importantly, *not* pregnant. Whereas *she* will never be worthy in his eyes. As she settles into one of the cheap seats, the bus lurches forward and her heart falls. She real-izes she will never live up to his standards. Exhausted emotionally and physically, she wonders what her future holds.

She recalls the year her family fell apart. It was at the tender age of thirteen when both her grandmother and mother passed away within months of each other. No one talked about it. It wasn't allowed. It was as if the topic avoided would alleviate their pain. Instead, the silence and void led to devastating effects.

After the deaths, her father grew more hateful and critical, often withdrawing to his room. Her sister headed out on her own, making a new life for herself. Her older brother became obsessed with sex at this time, sneaking into her bedroom occasionally to awaken her with his hands on her body. She shuddered at the thought, recalling the feel of his breath, moist and heavy, on her neck. Each time he'd visit, she'd cry, and each time, her brother would threaten, "Stop bawling, you big baby! I only touched you, not hurt you. You better get ready for a boyfriend. After all, that's what teenage boys do!"

As he'd push her away, his nostrils would flare and spit would fly from his mouth as he'd whisper in an angry voice, "You tell anyone and I'll kill you!"

The light from the outside pole shone through her bedroom window, making sure to spotlight the dreaded occasions along with her brother's profile. She hated that light and she hated her brother. She even hated her sister for not being there for her.

Falling into a deep depression after her mother's death, she feels as if a part of her heart has died along with her mother. As the years pass, she grows to look more like her mother, and she notices how her father becomes even more abusive toward her, while distancing himself emotionally.

Shattered and lonely, she begins to look for love "in all the wrong places," and like too many other young girls, she finds it. Falling head over heels for a young man of questionable character, she ignores the fact that their first encounter should have thrown up a red flag in their relationship. His eyes scanned her body up and down as he let out a long whistle while making inappropriate hand gestures. She—desperate for attention, any attention–was flattered. After all, as her brother informed her, isn't this what teenage boys were supposed to do?

It is his long, blonde hair that gives him an enticing "bad boy" appeal. His interest in her makes her feel special, especially after being discounted by her father and brother and dismissed by her sister. Zeroing in on her vulnerability, he uses flattery to win her over, and it isn't long before he pressures her into saying "yes" to physical intimacy. Sadly, she mistakes lust for his expression of love.

Taking advantage of her in every possible way, he soon begins to mistreat her verbally, emotionally, physically and sexually. On one particular date night, after their usual "sex session," he pinches her waist. "What's this? Looks like you're getting a bit pudgy. Maybe you need to slow down on those French fries." He pulls his t-shirt over his head and she pulls away, tears forming in her eyes.

Digging his shoes from the floorboard of the truck, he mockingly laughs. "Are you kiddin' me? You're gonna cry over that?" She gets out of the car, slamming the door as he continues to taunt her. "Oh, C'mon, Miss Piggy. Lighten up." He starts the car, threatening to drive away, so she jumps back in. She knows his temper, and realizing they are miles from nowhere, she doesn't wish to be stranded in the woods. To avoid further confrontation, she turns her face toward her window, hoping to ride home in silence.

Throughout the next couple of weeks, his comments grow more insulting, and she reaches her fill. Realizing he is just like the other men in her life, another abusive male, she calls it quits. "That's it," she demands one night when he attempts to take her parking *again*. "You want me for just one thing. I just can't do this anymore. I want you to take me home."

"What? You breakin' up with me? Who do you think you are? You ain't nothing but a slut. I could have any girl at the school, but I chose you. And you're gonna break up with me because I told you to lose some weight? I don't think so!" Again, she pulls away.

"See what I mean?" she cries.

For just a moment, he softens. "Oh, C'mon. I'm just kiddin! A little weight ain't no big thing. Just don't keep gainin'. That's all I'm sayin'." As she shakes her head and glares at him, he grabs her breast roughly. "You know you want it. Quit playin' around." He attempts to pull her shirt over her head, but she refuses. Angry, he rips it off and forces himself upon her. Afterward, when she's finally free, she reaches across the seat and slaps him.

His anger is fierce and she feels a blunt force across her own face in reciprocation. For a moment, she can't see and then she senses the puffiness around her eye. He touches her face, apologizing profusely. "Oh, baby! I'm so sorry. I didn't mean to do that. I just don't wanna lose you. I don't know what I'd do if I lost you." He kisses her cheek tenderly and this time, she stays put, too afraid to pull away.

When he drives up to drop her off, she slams the door in his face after jumping out. "That's it. We are done!" She runs into the house, praying he will let her go, but the loud revving up of his truck's engine, the expletives shouted out the window, and the smell of burnt rubber as his tires squealed out of the driveway, tells her he won't.

Her continued attempts to avoid him at school are only met with anger. Despite her pleas to be left alone, he stalks her the following week. When she refuses to go out with him again, he becomes more determined. Still, she is surprised when he comes banging on the front door late one evening.

"Go away!" she shouts through the door. "I don't want to see you anymore!" When she is met with silence, she hopes he has complied. Turning away, she hears glass shatter, and she knows before she even sees him, she is *not* safe. She yells out, attempting to run from him as he kicks his way through the broken window and grabs her by her hair. Throwing her down, he holds a knife to her throat, reminding her she used to be "his" girl. "You used to like it when I touched you like this," he whispers, holding the blade near her ear while groping her body with his free hand.

When she spits at his face, he becomes enraged. He rips her shorts off and as she cries out, the empty rooms echo her screams. "You think you're too good for me? Is that what you think?" He slaps her as she glares up at him, tears sliding down the sides of her face.

"I'll show you," he slurs with a drunken chuckle. "You'll see. When you have my baby, you'll know you ain't too good for me! You'll come crawling back to me then, won't you? Won't you?!" he demands, his breath reeking of alcohol. She tries to shove him off, but his weight is too great and she quickly realizes she is no match for his anger *or* his strength.

As he rolls away, she lies crying on the floor until he leaves. Crawling to the shower, she wonders what to do. She can't go to the police. This is small-town America and they had seen the two of them together numerous times. They wouldn't believe her. She definitely can't go to her dad or brother. Who knows how they would respond?!

She is too afraid to go to her friends. They might judge her. And her older sister had washed her hands of the family long ago!

She prays for someone to talk to; for God to send her help. Yet, when a teacher asks about the bruises on her wrist and face, she refuses to speak up, embarrassed by it all. She decides that it is better to stay silent; at least for now. Until she realizes she is pregnant with *his* child.

Feeling shameful, helpless, and desperate, she finally confides in her best friend. Sitting in her friend's car, they munch on burgers from the local Dairy Queen and make small talk. As she picks nervously at the sesame seed bun, she takes a tiny bite. Her friend takes notice. Seeing the worried frown on her face, her friend speaks up. "What's wrong? You've barely touched your food and you've been acting super stressed all week. What's going on?"

She blurts out, like a dam bursting when the weight of the water becomes too much, "I'm only sixteen-years-old and I'm pregnant!" She hangs her head shamefully. "I'm pregnant! I tried to stop him, but he was too strong for me!" she lets out a wail and stops to catch her breath before continuing. Her friend hands her a napkin to catch the snot running from her nose.

Finally, able to speak again, she continues. "I couldn't tell my dad. You know what he's like. He's going to kill me and then he's going to kill *him* if he finds out he raped me," she finished. "He never liked him anyway.

Reaching across the seat, her friend places her arm around her shoulder and squeezes, wishing she could take the fear from her. "I'm so sorry. I didn't know. So, you haven't told your dad yet?" As she shakes her head, her friend rolls her eyes and nods. "He is going to kill you! When do you plan to tell him?" The concern in her voice is evident. "How will he take it?"

She continues shaking her head, tears dripping onto her clasped hands. "I don't know. What am I going to do?" They hold hands, pray and cry together for the next hour.

She blows her nose on the flimsy napkin again, "I know my dad won't take it well, but he's bound to find out in a few months anyway, and then what?" She taps her tummy.

Her friend pats her back. "Let me go with you. I'll tell him for you," she offers.

"No." She shakes her head. "That might make it worse. I've just got to face the music and hope for the best. After a few more minutes of small talk, her friend drives her home. She gives her friend one more hug, dreading the moment she tells her father.

During the confession, her father listens stoically. Then he summons her to *his* bed. As he forces himself upon her, she cries until he stops. Disgusted with her, he pushes her away.

Awakened when the bus bounces over a rough patch on the highway, she realizes it's all still too true when emerging from *that* nightmare to her current painful existence. Still, she prefers it to reliving *that* scene again. Though the night air is warm and humid, *that* memory brings a chill that causes her body to shiver.

She stretches her legs under the seat in front of her, attempting to settle into her new reality. The stench of vomit and body odor fills her nostrils. She gags as the man in the seat across the aisle nurses a bottle of whiskey, tipping it towards her. Shaking her head vigorously at him, the anger and hurt overwhelm her. She is distraught and repulsed. As the drunkard gives her a two-toothed grin, she hugs her arms protectively around her body.

Remorse, hurt and fear erupt as she turns toward the window crying silently to God, just as her mother used to do. She dabs hastily at her eyes with a worn, snotty tissue. *"Where are you, Lord? Why won't you hear me? Why won't you help me?"* She cries, feeling unworthy of God's love, and unsure that He will answer.

The only response is the thump-thump-thump of the tires over the rough pavement, along with an occasional snore from the man across from her and the cry of the baby in front of her. The wailing only reminds her of her own predicament. Feeling her insides knot up, she pulls her knees to her chest and rests her head against the dusty window pane, fighting sleep as the bus jostles down the highway. She awakes again, hours later to find herself three states from home.

Stepping from the bus into unknown territory, she surprisingly manages to find her way to the stark office. "Fill out these forms," the lady with the brown bun on her head demands, unsympathetically. Dutifully, she does as she's told and hands the clipboard back to "Mrs. Brown Bun."

The lady squints while scanning the paperwork. Lowering her glasses, she then shakes her head, thinking what is about to be said will be upsetting. "Nope. You're too far along, honey. Sorry. We can't help you."

For a moment, she doesn't move. Leaning forward, she wants to be sure she heard Mrs. Brown Bun correctly.

"Didn't you hear me?" the lady asked again. As tears begin streaming down the young girl's face, Mrs. Brown Bun softens her voice. "You're too far along for an abortion. We'll have to send you to the unwed mothers' home, which is elsewhere. They'll take care of you there." Relieved, she can only nod as the lady hands her a tissue.

Her heart races as she boards the bus once more. This time, however, the dread is replaced with hope. *"He was listening! He did hear me! He does find me worthy. More importantly, He finds this little life inside of me worthy!"* She pats her belly and feels comforted, despite the long, tiring journey back east.

Resting her head on the back of the seat, she feels thankful, even though she was abandoned by her family and disowned by her father. She would soon hand this little bump in her belly to someone else to raise. She has been given another chance and this baby inside her will have life. She feels God's presence. She knows He has answered her cry. He has intervened on her behalf to provide a better way.

Just a few short months later, she is reminded to be thankful as she reluctantly hands over the pink, precious bundle. She prays for the baby she cannot raise. She prays for direction as she considers all the unknowns in her future. She prays for strength to face and forgive her father again. She prays for the stamina to finish her high school senior year.

She smiles knowing that God allowed her to give this child life through His intervention. She realizes she is no longer a slave to fear. Her faith reminds her how God will order her steps. He will make her broken life whole again and use her scarred past to bring glory to Him in her future.

As she swallows the huge lump in her throat, she knows that she will always have a Father who loves her for *who* she is. In her heavenly Father, she has found acceptance and love. She has found peace and she can rest in the knowledge that God will also guide the path of her new daughter. She is now, and forever will be, worthy in her Father's eyes.

Heart to Heart:

"I am he who blots out your transgressions
for my own sake, and I will not remember your sins."
Isaiah 43:25

What is keeping you from feeling worthy? Who has rejected you? What fears must you let go of in order to feel worthy in His eyes and allow God to have control of your life? How can you use the scars from the past to glorify God in the present and inspire others in the future?

_____

_____

_____

Chapter 6
Perfume and Pardon

"Jesus said to the woman,
"Your faith has saved you; go in peace."
Luke 7:50

The woman looked up in humble astonishment, feeling the incredible renewal and freedom she sought. Drawing back her damp hair, she raised a perfumed hand, unsure of how to thank Him.

Jesus' loving gaze contrasted with Simon's look of disgust. She ignored Simon and responded to her Savior as He gave her freedom from the shame that had followed her into this room. That shame remained at Jesus' feet as she left Him to go on her way.

Simon gasped, wondering how *this* woman, *this* sinner, *this* "lady of the evening" could be forgiven. *What audacity! How dare she show her face here! How could she dare seek compassion?!*

Even more so, Simon was appalled at Jesus. *How could he offer this woman redemption? Did he not know who she was?!* Recounting the events of the hour, this Pharisee host wondered how the afternoon changed so suddenly.

The quiet evening started with Jesus reclining at the low table, partaking of a meal as a guest with Simon, the Pharisee and his friends. The meal was interrupted by a small commotion when the woman entered.

She had learned of Jesus' presence here. He was the Messiah who was said to have healed the blind, made the lame to walk again and forgave sinners. She wanted this same man, *this* Jesus, to make her life new and to bring wholeness to her heart. In exchange, she brought him her most prized possession; an expensive flask of perfume.

Knowing her purpose, she paused before Jesus to see how He would receive her. Smiling kindly, He continued to recline as she approached. Tears began to stream from her eyes and she wondered how His simple gaze had caused such emotion. Feeling unworthy, she fell at His feet and sobbed, her tears spilling onto His feet. Pulling her long tresses from behind her shoulders, she wiped His feet, cleaning them before the anointment.

Jesus did not prohibit this action, but Simon's indignation was evident. *Doesn't He know who is touching Him? How could He allow such a woman—such a sinner—to put her hands on Him? Perhaps He was not who He said He was. Perhaps He was not a prophet after all or He would not consent to her waste of such a precious commodity.*

Jesus ignored Simon and gently touched the face of the weeping woman. Her tears fell more freely at this gesture, and she began to kiss His feet, not caring if they were dirty and bruised. Experiencing His love, warmth and forgiveness, her emotions poured through her tears and the perfume which she lavished upon his feet. The fragrance filled the room, causing Simon to scoff more openly.

Then Jesus, knowing Simon's thoughts, declared, "Simon, I have something to say to you."

Surprised, Simon nodded. "Speak, Teacher."

"A certain lender had two debtors. One owed five hundred silver coins, and the other fifty. When they could not pay, the lender cancelled the debt of both. Now, which of them will be most grateful? Which will love the lender more?" Jesus asked.

Annoyed at such a question, Simon responded, "The one who has the larger debt, of course!"

Jesus replied, "You are right." Pausing, He gestured toward the woman. "Do you see this woman?"

Without speaking, Simon squinted and rolled his eyes. He shook his head in a condescending manner. *Of course, I see her. I know who she is. Don't you? Don't you see what she is? Some prophet you are!*

Jesus continued. "When I came into your home, you offered no water to wash my feet. Yet, she has wet my feet with her tears and wiped them with her hair. You did not greet me with a kiss, but she has not ceased to kiss my feet. You failed to anoint my head with oil, but she has anointed my *feet* with perfume. Therefore, her sins, which are many, are forgiven—for she *loved* that much." Jesus looked to the woman and then back at Simon. "He who is forgiven little, loves little." He turned back to the woman before continuing, "Your sins are forgiven."

Simon's face flushed with shame. Simon's dinner guests at the table were embarrassed for Simon. They began to grumble and whisper among themselves. "Who is this, that thinks *he* can forgive sin?"

Jesus paid them no mind. He continued speaking to the woman, as He lifted her face to meet His gaze. "Your faith has saved you; go in peace."

The woman looked up in humble astonishment, feeling the incredible renewal and freedom she had sought. Her flask empty, her earthly fortune gone, her heart feels full. She leaves the alabaster container and rises slowly to her feet. She has discovered something much sweeter than her perfume. She has discovered pardon. Redeemed, loved and now acknowledged by the Almighty, she inhales His acceptance into every fiber of her being. Lingering just long enough to smile gratefully at Jesus, she ducks out of Simon's house, a new and grateful woman (Luke 7:36-50).

Heart to Heart:

Jesus is waiting patiently to provide you with the sweetness of His peace, the gift of His grace, the healing of your heart. There is no need to barter with your prized possessions. Jesus has already paid a very heavy price for you. Just leave your cares before Him and confess His name to receive Him. What shame will you drop at Jesus' feet today? What pardon do you need? How will you allow God to help you feel worthy through His forgiveness, His acknowledgement and His vast, eternal love for you?

"I, even I, am He who blots out your transgressions,
for my own sake, and remembers your sins no more"
Isaiah 43:25

_____

_____

_____

Chapter 7
Your Turn:
Your Story ... Your Testament

"In him we have redemption through his blood, the forgive-
ness of sins, in accordance with the riches of God's grace."
Ephesians 1:7

After reading about the lives of six different women, you can see how God provided *Grace* to each, along with a spiritual and emotional healing. He offers those same gifts to you. You don't have to earn them. You don't have to be deserving of them. You don't have to die for them. You just need to accept Him.

His gifts are free. Jesus paid that price for all ... with His blood, with His life, with His love! He cares that much for YOU!

Consider where you are in your journey. Have you already experienced Jesus' forgiveness, love and peace? Or, are you allowing a sense of unworthiness to hold you back? Is there guilt or shame that is weighing you down ... attempting to define and limit your life? If so, confess your sins before Jesus and invite Him into your life. As Romans 3:23 tells us, *"For all have sinned and fallen short of the glory of God."*

Next, read John 3:16, "For God so loved the world that He gave His only begotten Son that whosoever believes in Him will not perish but have everlasting life." Profess your belief through your testimony that Jesus is the Christ, the Son of the Living God, who died for us and rose again so that we might have eternal life with Him.

Trust that He can and will strengthen and guide you. Remember that you never need to earn God's love and forgiveness. He has freely given it. It is yours for the asking. Yours for receiving.

Finally, remember this. Whatever your experiences or circumstances, you have a story to tell. You have a testimony to share. How has God moved in your life? How have you allowed Jesus to help you release the shame and guilt and choose a new way of living and loving? To walk with confidence with Him? How have you forgiven yourself through His forgiveness?

Look over the notes you wrote in each Heart to Heart section. What story is God calling you to share? Pray and allow God to help you write your testimony. When you finish, go to the final section of this chapter, "Using Your Testimony," and consider taking those additional steps.

As you move forward in this life, it's important to remember that you are on a journey. You will continue to face trials. You will continue to fall down. You will continue to make mistakes.

More importantly, know that Jesus is with you always. He will pick you up when you stumble. He will provide His peace during anxious times. He will bring joy where there is sorrow. He will never leave you, nor forsake you. Remember there is no sin too great that His grace and love can't and won't cover. Last, but certainly not least, find a group of other believers to support and walk with you on your journey. We were not made to walk this earth alone, as we are reminded in Ecclesiastes 4:9-12, "Two are better than one, because they have a good return for their labor. If either of them falls down, one can help the other up … Though one may be overpowered, two can defend themselves. A cord of three strands is not quickly broken."

Start writing your story now …

_____

_____

_____

_____

_____

_____

_____

_____

_____

_____

_____

_____

_____

_____

_____

_____

_____

_____

_____

_____

_____

_____

_____

_____

_____

_____

_____

_____

_____

_____

_____

_____

_____

_____

_____

_____

_____

_____

_____

_____

_____

_____

_____

_____

_____

_____

_____

_____

_____

_____

Using Your Testimony:

Though the reading of this book may be complete, writing and sharing your story is not. Consider how you might serve as a vessel for the Lord with your testimony. How can you use *this* as an opportunity to encourage others and glorify His name? To help someone else come to know Christ and His grace? How will you help that person to write and share her story? Or his story?

1. Think of someone you know who needs God's healing. Write that person's name here: _____

2. When and where will you meet with this person? _____
_____

3. How will you share the message of God along with your own testimony to support their healing? Write down your plan: _____
_____
_____

4. What else will you need to do to support this person? To inspire her/him to write a testimony and in turn, reach out to others to do the same? What follow up might be needed and what will that look like?

_____
_____
_____
_____
_____
_____
_____
_____